LOVE/STORIES
(OR, BUT YOU WILL GET USED TO IT)

LOVE/STORIES (OR, BUT YOU WILL GET USED TO IT)

⊰ FIVE SHORT PLAYS ⊱

ITAMAR MOSES

NORTHWESTERN UNIVERSITY PRESS

EVANSTON, ILLINOIS

Northwestern University Press
www.nupress.northwestern.edu

Printed in the United States of America

10 9 8 7 6 5 4 3 2 1

LIBRARY OF CONGRESS CATALOGING-IN-PUBLICATION DATA

Moses, Itamar, 1977–
    Love/stories, or, But you will get used to it : five short plays / Itamar Moses.
        p. cm.
    ISBN 978-0-8101-2691-6 (pbk. : alk. paper) 1. Love—Drama. I. Title.
II. Title: Love/stories. III. Title: But you will get used to it.
    PS3613.O77889L68 2010
    812.6—dc22

                                                                    2009044643

∞ The paper used in this publication meets the minimum requirements of the American National Standard for Information Sciences—Permanence of Paper for Printed Library Materials, ANSI Z39.48-1992.

To Michelle, with pregnant silence

CONTENTS

Production History *ix*

Cast of Characters *xiii*

One: *Chemistry Read* 5

Two: *Temping* 23

Three: *Authorial Intent* 31

Four: *Szinhaz* 67

Five: *Untitled Short Play* 85

PRODUCTION HISTORY

Prior to their ever being presented together, some portions of *Love/Stories* were first produced separately:

Authorial Intent was originally commissioned by Liz Engelman for the McCarter Theatre, Princeton, N.J. (Emily Mann, artistic director), and was first presented there in a staged reading as part of their Short Play Festival, on October 19, 2004, directed by Barbara Rubin. The cast was as follows:

A . . . . Jennifer Erin Roberts
B . . . . Duane Boutté

Authorial Intent had its world premiere as half of the double-bill Authorial Intent/Idea at Manhattan Theatre Source, New York City, on April 10, 2005. The production was directed by Michelle Tattenbaum. The stage manager was Amber Estes. The cast was as follows:

A . . . . Ami Shukla
B . . . . Gideon Banner

Untitled Short Play had its world premiere as a part of The Mag 7, an evening of short plays produced by Naked Angels (Jenny Gersten, artistic director), at the Flea Theater, New York City, on February 16, 2006. The play was directed by Michelle Tattenbaum, with set design by Faye Armon, lighting design by Ben Tevelow, costumes by Daphne Javitch, and sound by Brittany O'Neill. The production stage manager was Rhonda Picou. The cast was as follows:

Man .... Michael Crane
Woman .... Erin McMonagle
The Reader .... Gideon Banner

Szinhaz had its world premiere as a part of Armed and Naked in America, an evening of short plays produced by Naked Angels (Jenny Gersten, artistic director), at the Duke Theater, New York City, on April 11, 2007. The play was directed by Michelle Tattenbaum, with set design by David Rockwell, lighting design by Jason Lyons, costumes by Jessica Wegener, sound by Tony Smolenski IV and Drew Levy, and props by Jeremy Lydic and Matthew Hodges. The production stage manager was Cole Bonenberger. The cast was as follows:

Marie .... Bess Wohl
Istvan .... Brian Avers

Love/Stories (or, but you will get used to it) had its world premiere at the Flea Theater, New York City (Jim Simpson, artistic director; Carol Ostrow, producing director), on February 16, 2009. The production was directed by Michelle Tattenbaum, with set design by Jerad Schomer, lighting design by Joe Chapman, costumes by Jessica Pabst, and sound by Brandon Wolcott. The assistant director was Nicole Rosner. The production stage manager was Amanda Pooran.

The cast was as follows:

Man One . . . . Michael Micalizzi
Man Two . . . . Felipe Bonilla
Man Three . . . . John Russo
Woman One . . . . Laurel Holland
Woman Two . . . . Maren Langdon
Understudies: Marc LeVasseur, Dorien Makhloghi, Jessica Pohly, Erin Roth, Stephen Stout

CAST OF CHARACTERS

All roles are performed by a total of three men and two women.

Man One plays: Actor Two (*Chemistry Read*),
Guy (*Temping*), B (*Authorial Intent*)

Man Two plays: Writer (*Chemistry Read*),
Istvan (*Szinhaz*), Man (*Untitled Short Play*)

Man Three plays: Actor One (*Chemistry Read*),
The Reader (*Untitled Short Play* [and in all transitions])

Woman One plays: Actress (*Chemistry Read*),
A (*Authorial Intent*), Woman (*Untitled Short Play*)

Woman Two plays: Director (*Chemistry Read*),
Girl (*Temping*), Marie (*Szinhaz*)

A note about the text that follows: All five of the plays in this collection were written to be, and on many occasions have been, performed on their own or in tandem with short plays by various other authors. In order to make it as easy as possible both to reproduce *Love/Stories* as a complete event and for the plays to continue their individual lives, text for a character, The Reader, is provided (on its own page, before each play) to serve as a transition between plays when they are performed together. To perform a play individually simply omit this text.

LOVE/STORIES
(OR, BUT YOU WILL GET USED TO IT)

[*A man, the* READER, *appears.*]

READER: Love Stories. [*Beat.*] Love.

[*He makes a slashing gesture.*]

    Stories.
    Or: But You Will Get Used to It.
    One. Chemistry Read.

[*A transition begins as the scene he describes begins to form . . .*]

READER: Lights up on a man, in a room, auditioning for a play. He has just finished delivering a short monologue.

ONE

CHEMISTRY READ

[*A* DIRECTOR *and a* WRITER *sit behind a table, facing* ACTOR ONE, *who is holding audition sides. Off to one side is an* ACTRESS *seated at a music stand.*]

DIRECTOR: Thank you.

ACTOR ONE: I, oh, that's it?

DIRECTOR: Yeah, no, yes. I've . . . seen all I need to see.

ACTOR ONE: Oh. Okay.

DIRECTOR: I mean, we're really not having people do the whole thing.

ACTOR ONE [*pointing at* WRITER]: I mean, I really love the writing. [*Pointing at* ACTRESS] And I'd love to also do the part with—

DIRECTOR: *I* don't need to see anything else right now.

[*She turns to* WRITER.]

Unless . . . ?

WRITER: Uh . . . Yeah, I'd like to see him read with her, sure.

DIRECTOR: Um. Okay. Keep going.

ACTOR ONE: Okay! Uh . . .

[*He looks down at the text. A moment.*]

Just trying to find a place to . . . Jesus, this speech is all one sentence, isn't it?

DIRECTOR: Yes. Yes it is.

ACTOR ONE: I'll . . . Okay. Yeah.

[*He looks at* ACTRESS. *A moment. Then:*]

". . . and that now could turn around, and see light."

[*As* ACTOR ONE *plays the scene, he isn't cartoonishly bad. But he doesn't nail it. Maybe the note is this: whereas it would be effective to play a kind of endearing nervousness in the reality of the scene, he instead seems endearingly nervous, and therefore awkward and stumbly, about the audition itself.*]

ACTRESS: "That's really sweet."

ACTOR ONE: "Well it's true."

ACTRESS: "And, look, it's not that I don't think you're totally amazing, too, I do, I mean, you're saying all this great stuff, and I'm not reciprocating? But it's only because I don't, um. I don't want to send you mixed messages."

ACTOR ONE: "You're in my apartment and on my couch."

ACTRESS: "Should I go? Do you want me to go?"

ACTOR ONE: "No I don't want you to go. I want you to stay."

ACTRESS: "Okay. Or, I mean, I can't *stay* stay. I can stay for a *while.* But I can't, like, *stay.*"

ACTOR ONE: "Well okay but last week—"

ACTRESS: "Right and I told you I wasn't sure that was a good idea. So—"

ACTOR ONE: "Ah, well, *I* don't think it's a good idea for you to leave *tonight,* so—"

ACTRESS: "Very funny."

ACTOR ONE: "Look, I . . . I don't think you've really given this a chance? Like, not enough of a chance, not really, I mean, we don't even really know what this *is* yet, so . . . I would love it. If you'd stay."

[*A moment.*]

DIRECTOR: Nice. Really nice.

WRITER: *Really* nice.

DIRECTOR: Just lovely, yeah. [*Beat.*] *Thank* you.

ACTOR ONE: Thank *you.*

DIRECTOR: Yeah, no, thanks for coming in. It's always good to see you.

ACTOR ONE [*to* DIRECTOR]: Good to see you too. [*To* WRITER] Nice to meet you. [*To* ACTRESS] Thank you. Uh. "Pleasure working with you." [*Generally*] Thanks for bringing me in. Have a good one.

[ACTOR ONE *exits. A moment.*]

DIRECTOR: Poor guy!

WRITER: Hey—

DIRECTOR: I'd love to do the part with her.

WRITER: Just, hey, come on, he just wanted a chance to show more.

DIRECTOR: The first time I directed a show? I didn't know that "thank you" was the magic phrase at auditions that meant go away. So I would just say thank you after anybody did anything even if I wanted them to stay and act more. I couldn't figure out why everybody kept leaving.

WRITER: Heh.

[*Beat.*]

DIRECTOR: Okay so I think that's it. I'll just go make sure there's nobody still . . . And then we can, you know, make our final—

WRITER: Okay.

DIRECTOR: Okay.

[DIRECTOR *goes. A silence.* WRITER *looks at* ACTRESS. *They smile awkwardly then look away. Then she speaks.*]

ACTRESS: *Thank* you.

WRITER: I, what?

ACTRESS: Thank *you,* by the way, for calling me in to do this, it's—

WRITER: Oh, I didn't.

ACTRESS: No, I know, I meant "you" like "you guys" like "whoever thought of me."

WRITER: The director, I think she knew you, so—

ACTRESS: I mean, a lot of actors don't like doing it? They think being a reader for auditions is sort of thankless? Which it is? In that you're sitting there doing the scene again and again but not actually really being considered for the part and meanwhile you're seeing all these actors who *are* being considered and a lot of them are terrible and you're, like, oh, am I actually worse than all of these people? *But.* It's also kind of a good reminder, you know, just being *present,* for so long, for so many people, in a row, it's more about listening, about supporting, all the things actors should do, but they don't, because it's not the flashy stuff, you know?

WRITER: Uhh—

ACTRESS: And it's just useful, too. To see it from this side. You learn *a lot*. About, especially . . . [*Pointing after* AC-TOR ONE] About what *not* to do.

WRITER: Mm.

ACTRESS: Hey, so is this play *about* someone in particular?

WRITER: I, *what?*

ACTRESS: Or, no, that's, if that's—

WRITER: I, no, no no no, it's okay, it's, um . . . [*Beat.*] You know, it's all sort of, everything kind of . . . [*Beat.*] You sort of take everything and—

ACTRESS: But so it's not about, like, the love of your life, who you're still with? That you wrote as like an incredibly romantic *gift* to her?

WRITER: Ha. Um. Aha. No. No no. [*Beat.*] No, the girl who I was sort of thinking of when I . . . She *totally* . . . [*Beat.*] And I hear she's with some *actor* now, so—

ACTRESS: Ew.

WRITER: I know, but so. No. No.

[*Beat. He looks at* ACTRESS *anew.*]

So you—

[DIRECTOR *returns, handing* WRITER *a headshot.*]

DIRECTOR: Hey, sorry, turns out we've got one more.

WRITER: Oh God.

DIRECTOR: He thought he wouldn't be able to come, but he moved some things, blah blah blah, anyway—

[*During this,* DIRECTOR *sits back down and gestures toward the door. Meanwhile,* ACTOR TWO *has entered, holding the audition sides.* WRITER *who has been staring at the headshot, dismayed, looks up and is more dismayed, seeing the same face in the flesh.*]

ACTOR TWO: Hey, sorry, I know you guys are at the end of your day, and I'm not even on your list, because I didn't—

[*Perhaps* ACTOR TWO *slings his bag to the floor like he owns the room.*]

DIRECTOR: No, it's fine.

WRITER [*simultaneously*]: Yeah we don't really have—

ACTOR TWO: I just, I thought I wasn't going to be able to come in, but I *love* the script, my girlfriend told me about your writing, I guess she knows you? But yeah I *love* it, I just *love* it, so I moved some, anyway, I hope it's okay.

DIRECTOR: It's fine, it's great.

ACTOR TWO: But so I'll just jump right in, because I know you're . . .

[*He looks at* ACTRESS.]

Okay? Okay. "I wrote something about you. Do you want to hear it?"

ACTRESS: "Okay."

[*During* ACTOR TWO'*s audition,* WRITER *slowly begins to engage in a subtle but gradually escalating series of distractions, perhaps clicking his pen or dropping his pen or shifting in his chair or clearing his throat or laughing at an odd moment or whatever is organic. Perhaps the* DIRECTOR *glances at him disapprovingly during this. Regardless, throughout,* ACTOR TWO *manages to continue his audition, mostly undisturbed, and is actually quite good.*]

ACTOR TWO: "I knew, from the moment that I saw you I just knew, I had that sort of puzzle-piece click of rightness or of recognition, such that part of me woke up, and thought, oh yes, that's right, I had forgot this feeling, the one that touches you at last someplace in which you didn't even know you were still sad, until, having been touched, the sadness moves and is dislodged, as though you, as though the simple sight of you, was some bright tool of surgical precision, shaped exactly so to wedge beneath my sadness, and pry it out, release what was pent up back there, what was blocked off, or all that time faced backwards, and that now could turn around, and see light."

ACTRESS: "That's really—"

WRITER: *Thank* you.

ACTOR TWO: I, oh, that's it?

WRITER: That is *all* I need to see.

ACTOR TWO: Okay.

WRITER: We're not really having people do the whole thing.

[*There is a lot of overlapping throughout the following.*]

DIRECTOR: Well, but—

WRITER: *Thank* you, though.

DIRECTOR: Actually—

ACTOR TWO: Okay. Nice to meet you, I really, again I *love* the script.

DIRECTOR: Um—

WRITER: Mhm.

ACTOR TWO [*to* DIRECTOR]: Always good to see you.

DIRECTOR: Uh, you too. In fact, actually—

WRITER [*to* ACTRESS]: And thank *you.* Too. For the day. Thanks.

ACTRESS: Oh, okay.

[ACTRESS *starts to collect her belongings.*]

DIRECTOR [*to* ACTRESS]: No, hold on—

ACTOR TWO [*to* ACTRESS]: Oh, yeah, thank you. Uh. "Pleasure working with you." [*Generally*] Thanks for letting me, uh—

DIRECTOR [*to* ACTOR TWO]: Would you . . . Actually?

[*A moment. She has finally succeeded in getting everyone's attention.*]

Would you stay? Or, I mean, would you just hang out, outside, for a bit?

ACTOR TWO: Oh! [*Beat.*] Oh, because he just said—

DIRECTOR: Yeah, no, we just . . . Sorry to send . . . Could you just give us a second?

ACTOR TWO: Of course. I'll . . . Yeah. Yes. Uh . . .

[ACTOR TWO *exits. A moment.*]

ACTRESS: So should I—?

DIRECTOR: Don't go anywhere. [*To* WRITER] What was that?

WRITER: *Oh*, did you, uh . . . ? Did you *like* him?

DIRECTOR: I was interested to see some more, yeah.

WRITER: Huh. See I, uh . . . I didn't really . . . *see* it. You know? *It.* You know?

DIRECTOR: Well, okay. How about we bring him back in and let him read again.

WRITER: Well we saw him read.

DIRECTOR: Yes we did. And I thought that he was good. But I'd like to do the chemistry read, see how he plays off the girl, or, you know, we don't have the *real* girl, but so we can at least—

WRITER: Look, look. I just . . . I just don't think that he's the right guy. Okay?

DIRECTOR: Well I think, of all the guys we saw today, he's the one I'm most interested in.

WRITER: Oh.

DIRECTOR: Yeah, so—

WRITER: *Why?*

DIRECTOR: What?

WRITER: Based on *that?*

DIRECTOR: Based on *what?*

WRITER: On him, like, reading a small part of the play? One time?

DIRECTOR: You mean auditioning?

WRITER: Well—

DIRECTOR: Because that's what auditioning *is*.

WRITER: Well, I mean, you know, uh, *exactly*, because it's a different skill, auditioning is a totally different skill, and, it, you know what? It actually, I actually, it actually makes me a little suspicious? When someone auditions really well? You know? Like it's sort of a *rule* of mine. Actually. Is: Never cast the person who gives the best audition. [*Beat.*] Yeah. [*Beat.*] Because then that's all he gives you, see, is that one performance, over and over, and you try to get him to deepen, or complicate, and he resists, or falls apart, and you'll be sorry, you'll be very very sorry. Trust me.

[*Beat.*]

DIRECTOR: I'm going to go out there now? And apologize on your behalf? And then I'm going to give him some notes, an adjustment or two, to think about? And then I'm going to come back in here to make sure you're ready? And then I'm going to bring him back in. Okay?

[*Beat.*]

WRITER: You know what? Do whatever you want.

[*A moment.* DIRECTOR *goes. A moment.*]

ACTRESS: All right, so, I guess I'll—

16

WRITER: Please help me.

ACTRESS: What?

WRITER: You have to help me.

ACTRESS: What? With what?

WRITER: I cannot cast that guy.

ACTRESS: Okay. Uh. Why?

WRITER: Because that's the guy! That's the fucking guy!

ACTRESS: Oh.

WRITER: Yeah. So, that's sort of just *there*, in my head, you know, like, why him, or what did I do, or not do, or what did *he* do, or not do, and and and but, and this isn't even *comforting*, but you know what it is *really*, is, what it *is* is . . . [*Beat.*] And I get it, you know? I get it. Everyone is drawn to, you know, whatever they happen to *respond* to because of, whatever, and it's not necessarily, like, a *reflection* on, of, on, and that's great, that is just great, I totally get that, but I am not then obliged also to *employ* him, am I? Of *course* not. Right?

[*Beat.*]

ACTRESS: Uhhhh . . .

[DIRECTOR *returns.*]

DIRECTOR: He's outside. He's waiting outside. Can I bring him back in?

[*A silence.*]

WRITER: I—

ACTRESS: I worked with him.

[*Beat.*]

DIRECTOR: What?

ACTRESS: Sorry, I, sorry, I mean I would have spoken up sooner, but I um . . . [*Beat.*] But, yeah, we did a show, and he was, yes, very very difficult. To work with. I mean, really dynamite, at first, really, whatever, like he showed you today, but then after that, just totally stagnant, like, nothing really beyond the surface once you scratched it, and really selfish, too, also, like did not make anybody else feel good, that he was working with, or, ultimately, look good, when we were up there, you know, when it actually counted, and but then not really possible to communicate with, you know? To improve anything that was going wrong? And so it was just this total disaster that everybody ultimately regretted being involved in. [*Beat.*] On top of which to make it worse he had replaced this other guy? Who'd been in the role before? Who, I mean, in retrospect, he was great, but he got let go, like, just a little ways into rehearsal because,

I don't even know, but which pretty quickly it became obvious had been a mistake. Because he hadn't done anything wrong. Except, like, have a little bit of a different, like, process? Which we didn't realize we probably would have preferred. Until he was gone. [*Beat.*] And, I mean, I don't know, obviously, that was just my one experience at, like, at one particular time, but, uh. There it is.

[*Beat.*]

DIRECTOR: I'll get rid of him.

[DIRECTOR *goes.*]

WRITER: Thank you.

ACTRESS: Oh.

[ACTRESS *starts to leave.*]

WRITER: No.

ACTRESS: Yeah, no, I gotta—

WRITER: Hey.

ACTRESS: It was, uh, thanks for—

WRITER: Hey!

ACTRESS: What?

[*A moment.* ACTRESS *has stopped at the door.*]

WRITER: Would you stay?

[*A moment.* ACTRESS *turns back around.*]

[*The* READER *appears again.*]

READER: Two. Temping.

[*A transition begins as the new scene he describes begins to form . . .*]

READER: Lights up on an office. A guy and a girl sit at neighboring desks. She is talking on the phone.

TWO

TEMPING

[*In an office, a* GUY *works at his desk, and a* GIRL *sits at neighboring desk. She is talking on the phone. He is working, collating piles of paper and then stapling them. Though* GUY *continues to work, he is very much listening to, and invested in, the details of her conversation.*]

GIRL: Yeah . . . Yeah . . . Yeah . . . Yeah . . . Yeah . . . Yeah . . . Yeah . . . Yeah . . . Well whenever it's convenient for you, I mean, there isn't much, and it's nothing I need right away, so there's no rush but, yeah, just to get it out of your way, I could, you know, any evening this week, really, I could, I mean, you know, not *any* evening this week, I just mean, since evenings are when you're usually . . . Oh . . . Oh, uh, why not? . . . Oh! When? . . . Oh, well that will be fun I mean you always said you wanted to do that at some point, so, that's great, I mean, it's great that you're doing that, and that's going to be in the evenings? . . . And, I mean, are you starting that right away, or, like . . . Oh. Why's that? . . . Oh. When are you leaving? . . . Cool . . . And are you going alone? . . . I said are you going alone? . . . Oh! No, yeah, that's cool, you guys will have fun, that's totally great. And they're just giving you the time off to . . . Oh . . . Well I mean cool. You've always, uh, you've always wanted to do that too. Well, look, why don't you tell me then what would be a good time . . . What? . . . What? . . . No. I don't . . . No. I'm not . . . Well I'm not . . . Well I said that I'm not so . . . Well okay I don't know I mean you're talking about all this stuff and I just kind of feel like the like hidden message of it is, you know, hey, now that we broke up, I'm free, I'm free to like go on this big trip with my friend, and to do all this stuff, like you couldn't do it when we were together, like you were in prison for three years and now you're out . . . I know, I know you didn't, but . . . I'm just saying that that's how it *feels*, from your voice, and the way that you're saying it . . . But you asked, you asked, I wasn't gonna . . . Oh well great so now you're deciding that too . . . No, look, I, fine, maybe we shouldn't, maybe we shouldn't, but we both agreed at least to try, and now it just seems like at like the first small problem, you're just, like, deciding that we shouldn't, or even . . . No never mind . . . No never mind . . . I said never mind . . . I was, okay, I was gonna say, or even like you're trying to create this problem, like, on purpose, to come up with a *reason* . . . I don't know . . . I don't know. I don't know either . . . Well maybe you could try to come up with something . . . No, you come up with something . . . Um, I don't know, but, like, for instance, why don't you instead of yelling at me try to make me feel at least a tiny bit better . . . Um. Oh . . . No, fine, fuck you, totally, fuck you, completely, fuck you too.

[GIRL *slams down the phone and immediately brings her hand to her mouth to stifle sobs. She takes a deep breath. She takes another. But actually she's crying. It's loud. Maybe she organizes some papers into a pile and stops after a few seconds. Maybe she clicks around on the desktop of her computer but stops after a few seconds. Throughout this,* GUY *perhaps hesitantly opens his mouth a couple of times to say something, perhaps turns partly toward her, but is always cowed by a new outbreak of sobbing. Finally, he thinks better of intruding and turns back to his work and staples some more papers, at which point* GIRL *speaks.*]

Oh my god could you do that any fucking louder.

GUY: What? I, what? No, I mean, yeah, I, I'm just—

GIRL: Shut up shut up you useless fucking temp.

GUY: Okay. Sorry, I—

GIRL: Shut up.

GUY: I, sorry.

[*A beat. Then, determinedly, the* GIRL *picks up the phone, dials, and waits.* GUY *now contents himself with simply collating papers, leaving the stapling for later. And once again he takes in what transpires during the conversation.*]

GIRL: Hey are you busy? . . . No, I'm okay, I'm okay . . . Well I just talked to him . . . I know . . . I know, but we . . . I know, but we said we would, and I don't know, it was fine, at first it was fine, I mean, we were just talking and it was totally normal, I swear, and I felt fine, I felt completely fine, we were even talking about, like, when I would come by to get the last of my stuff, and it was no big deal, it didn't even make me sad, it was just, like, *logistics*, and then . . . and then . . .

[*She starts to choke up a little.*]

No I'm okay I'm okay but just so *then* I'm like why don't I come by in the evening and he's like that's not good so I'm thinking oh my god he's, yeah, I know, I know, but that's not what it is, it's, he's going back to school, so I'm like, all right, cool, but so then when does that start, and he's like, not for a while, because he's going on this road trip with his good friend, which he's always said he wanted to do, and, which, oh, by the way, he also quit his job, and I'm like, oh that's totally cool, *just* like that, *just* like I *just* said it to you, and he's like, uh, what, and I'm like, what, and he's like *what*, and I'm like WHAT, and he's like you sound mad, you sound mad, is something wrong, is something wrong, is something wrong, and I was like, well, okay, I mean, if you really want to know, it's just, the way you're talking about all this stuff, and it's great, and but the whole tone of it is just like, now that I'm not with you anymore, I can really live my life, like I was holding you back, and he was like, well, if you're gonna be hypersensitive to everything I say then maybe we shouldn't be like talking at all anymore, and I was like, okay, *or you* could try to make me *feel* better. And do you know what he said? He said . . . He said . . .

[*She chokes up. She almost can't get it out.*]

He said that's the point. He said that's the point. He said that's not his job anymore. Not his job anymore! Like I had *hired* him! To take care of my feelings! And he quit! . . . I know . . . I know . . . No I know, that's true, I know that, of course I know that . . . Yeah . . . Yeah . . . Yeah . . . Yeah . . . Yeah . . . Yeah . . . Yeah . . . Yeah . . . Yeah . . . Yeah. No. I know. And thanks. Thank you . . . Well no seriously . . . No, I know, but thanks . . . I will . . . I will . . . I will . . . Okay. Bye.

[GIRL *hangs up. She takes a few deep breaths. Perhaps she rearranges her desk a little. Breathes. Better.* GIRL *looks over at* GUY. *This time,* GUY *remains focused steadfastly on his work. A moment.*]

I'm also a temp.

[*Beat.*]

GUY: Yeah?

GIRL: Yeah.

GUY: Oh. Uh. How long have you been here?

GIRL: Three years. [*Beat.*] But just. I'm sorry.

GUY: It's okay. [*Beat.*] I mean I can . . . staple . . . quieter, if you—

GIRL: No, you, no, you do that. As loud as you want. [*Beat.*] You're being *really* nice to me.

GUY: Oh well I mean, it's . . . [*Beat.*] I mean, we *all . . .* [*Beat.*] And *you*, you're, I mean, I know I don't, but *I* just think . . . [*Beat.*] I've *always* . . . [*Beat.*] I mean ever since—

[GIRL *jumps on* GUY *and starts making out with him.* GUY *is shocked but thrilled about this turn of events. They make out for a few moments, frantically. They probably knock things off the desk or something. Then, there's a moment where they just look at each other.* GIRL *touches* GUY's *face.*]

GIRL: You're so . . .

[*The phone on* GIRL's *desk rings. She freezes. It rings again. It rings a third time.* GIRL *dives back over to her desk and answers it.*]

Hello? Hello hello? . . . Hey . . . No I'm not . . . No. Nothing.

[GUY *has by now turned back to his work.* GIRL *glances over at him. But he is already looking away.*]

No.

[*The* READER *appears again.*]

READER: Three. Authorial Intent.

[*A transition begins as the lights fade . . .*]

READER: Darkness. A female voice speaks.

THREE

AUTHORIAL INTENT

1

[*In darkness, a recorded female voice speaks:*]

A [*recorded*]: One.

[*Lights up. The living room/kitchen of an apartment. A front door leads out toward the hall, and a hallway leads upstage back toward the unseen bedroom. Several partially unpacked boxes are here and there, neatly in corners for the most part. There is a closet door in one wall. Someone has just moved in, but the apartment is not messy. A is discovered seated on a stool, at a wraparound counter that separates the kitchen area from the living room area, looking into a small standing mirror she's placed on the counter, putting on makeup. Someone unlocks the front door. B enters from the hall, formally dressed, carrying a notebook.*]

A: Hey! How'd it go?

B: Worst night of my life.

A: What?

B: Can we open a window?

A: Are you hot?

B: No. I'm going to jump out of it.

[B *exits toward the bedroom.*]

A: Jesus. What happened?

B [*off*]: I don't want to talk about it.

A: You're not jumping out the window, are you? [*Pause.*] Hello? B?

[B *returns, without the notebook. He's removed his jacket and tie and now wears a T-shirt with his slacks.*]

B: What?

A: What happened?

B: I said I don't want to talk about it.

A: Okay.

[A *resumes attending to her makeup. A moment.*]

B: Okay, so, first of all, the place is packed, it's a pretty big lecture hall, but it's totally full, and I happen to know that not everybody got in who wanted to, so it's, I don't know, three hundred budding filmmakers are on the edges of their respective seats. And before he comes out, they give him this big introduction, right, like recapping his career? Which is of course amazing, and serves to remind us why we all aspire to *be* him, and why we're impatient to get to the part where he talks so that we can hang on his every word.

A: He wasn't good?

[B *is looking for something.*]

B: He was *brilliant,* of *course* he was brilliant I mean, what's kind of amazing about him, or, you know, *additionally* amazing, is the fact that he's that rare kind of person who combines real ability *at* something with a real ability to—

A: What are you looking for?

[*Beat.*]

B: Do you know where my slippers are?

A: I have no idea.

B: This is very disorienting. I just wanted the unpacking to be *over* so I did it really quickly, and now I cannot for the life of me find anything.

A: They'll turn up.

B: Do you mind if I just wear socks for now?

A: I . . . Why would I mind? Wear your socks.

B: *I* don't know. Now that we live together I expect to discover . . . all *kinds* of . . . Why are you looking at me like that?

A: Nothing, I just . . .

B: What?

A: Nothing.

B: Are you sure? Because—

A: So he was brilliant?

B: What? Oh. Yes. The *lecture* was great, complete with, you know, example clips and everything, making you see these scenes you thought you knew *so* well in like this totally new way, like, how behind everything, there's . . . And inside my head there's just lightbulbs going off left and right. Like when someone says something that you've always felt, instinctively, but have never been able to put into words? And then you hear it stated, and you're just like: yes yes yes.

A: Yes.

B: Right, so, *then* we get to: the question and answer section.

A: You didn't get to ask your question.

B: Would *that* make something the worst night of my life?

A: You are no stranger to melodrama.

B: I—

A: So what happened?

B: At first, usual stuff. People asking him to confirm anecdotes they heard, about funny things that happened on set, or where ideas came from, or about which of his movies is his favorite. Boring. But *then*. This one guy gets up and says, um, he says, "Are you happy?"

A: Excuse me?

B: Yeah, I know! This *guy* gets up and says, "Are you happy?"

A: Was it his conscience?

B: I know, right?

A: So what did he say?

B: He was quiet. For a long time. And then he says, "What do you mean?" And the guy says, "Does doing what you do make you happy?"

A: I guess . . . that's a good question.

B: I guess it was. Because he's quiet again for a while, and then he says, "Not in the way that I thought it would." And then he starts to talk. And he talks for maybe a half an hour, which is why I'm back so late, by the way, and he talks all about how, as a kid, he would go to see movies, and they would give him this wonderful feeling, really like nothing else, and he thought, "I want to do that. I want to get inside of that so that I can have that feeling all the time," and on and on and we're like,

"Where the hell is this going?" And then. He said the worst thing I have ever heard in my entire life.

A: What?

B: Hold on I have it written down.

[B *exits to the bedroom.*]

A: Why did you write it down? [*Pause.*] Why did you want to write down the worst thing you have ever heard in your entire life?

[B *returns with his notebook.*]

B: To, uh . . . I don't know. To take away its power?

A: Huh. [*Pause.*] So what is it?

B: He said [*reading*], "In order to do what I wanted to do for the rest of my life I had to learn so much about it that I ruined forever my ability to enjoy it in the way that made me want to do it in the first place."

[*Pause.*]

A: And?

B: And . . . what?

A: That's it? That's the worst thing you've ever heard in your life?

B: Don't you think that's depressing?

A: Yeah. For *him.*

B: For *all* of us.

A: Um. Only if it's *true* for all of us.

B: Well . . .

A: Well what?

B: Do you think it is?

A: No.

B: Why not?

A: Because that would be . . . *depressing.*

[*Beat.*]

B: Yeah, I'm going to need something better, because—

A: Can we not talk about this anymore?

B: Hey. All right. Of course.

A: It's just, you get in these *moods?* And I maybe don't feel like completely indulging that right now.

B: Oh. Okay. [*Beat.*] Are you upset about something? [*Beat.*] What are you doing?

A: I'm putting on makeup.

B: Yes, no, I see that you're putting on makeup, I just . . .
Well, for one thing, why are you doing it in the living
room?

A: The bathroom is all cluttered with your stuff.

B: Oh. [*Pause.*] I, uh . . . I haven't had time to find a place for
everything yet.

A: It's, no, it's fine, it's no rush, it's just that's why I'm out
here.

B: Oh. Okay. But . . . [*Pause.*] Shit. Right. Yes.

A: There it is.

B: I'm taking you out tonight. Oh, god, I'm sorry. I have to
get ready. I'm sorry I stayed so long at this thing, it's
just—

A: No, I know, he's your hero.

B: Well not anymore!

A: We don't have to *go* if you don't—

B: No, yes, yes, we're going out. I'm taking you to the the-
ater. See? Here. The tickets are on the bulletin board.
We're all set. And I can just throw back on my, uh . . .
God, I am *so* . . .

[B *exits into the bedroom.*]

A: It's fine!

B [*off*]: If I was still living on my own, you'd never have had to see this embarrassing moment of confusion. I'd have forgotten maybe, but *then* I'd have *remembered,* and you'd be none the wiser. But that's the risk, I guess. Exposure.

[B *returns, his jacket and button-down back on, tucking in his shirt, and restoring his tie.*]

A: It's completely fine.

B: Really?

A: Sweetie. It's totally fine.

[*A moment.* A *begins to cry.*]

B: *Hey.* [*Pause.*] Hey hey hey. What is it?

A: It's . . .

[*Pause.*]

B: What is it? What's wrong?

A: It's not fair.

B: What's not fair?

A: It's not *fair.*

B: Sweetie, what isn't?

A: Don't get *testy.* Don't get *testy* with me.

B: I'm not testy.

A: Don't *rush* me, then.

B: I'm not rushing you. [*Pause.*] What's not fair?

A: I'm trying to figure that out.

B: You're already crying about it.

A: Apparently.

B: So you know that something's unfair, you just don't know what it is yet.

A: *Yes.* I start crying and *then* I figure out why. That's how it *works* for me.

B: That's . . . *allowed.*

A: I mean, I know that's not how it works for *you.*

B: That's how it works for me sometimes.

A: Well I've never seen that.

B: Maybe you will now. Now that we live together.

[A *starts crying harder.*]

A [*because of the crying*]: Sorry . . . sorry . . .

B: Jesus, what the hell is wrong with you?

A: This isn't going to work.

B: Uh . . . What's not?

A: This was a mistake.

B: What was? The . . . choice of lipstick, or—

A: You moving in here. It was a terrible, terrible mistake.

[*Pause.*]

B: Oh.

A: Yeah. So.

B: What are you talking about? You, you can't know that yet, you can't—

A: I do. I *do* know it.

B: We've been living together three days.

A: So?

B: So . . . you can't *know* it's a mistake, what kind of . . . what *is* that?

A: It is.

B: But you can't *know* that. It's not . . . That doesn't make any *sense.*

A: I don't think that's really the point.

B: So what is the point?

A: That it's . . . It's all . . . going, it's evaporating, all of it. Already.

B: *What* is?

A: What I *feel* for you.

B: What are you *talking* about?

A: And because I can see that that's what's going to happen ... it's like it's gone already.

B: *What's* gone?

A: I, uh ... [*Pause.*] I don't love you.

B: What? [*Pause.*] Yes you do.

A: No.

B: Since ... Since *when*? Since ... ? Is this because I forgot for like a half a second that we were going *out* tonight?

A [*overlapping*]: No. No. Come on. Don't be ridiculous.

B: Oh, oh, *okay, I* will try to do *you* the courtesy of not being ridiculous in this conversation, yes, how, how *unfair* of me—

A: Don't be sarcastic. That's mean.

B: *I* ... ! *The* ... ! *You just* ... !

A: Don't shout at me.

B: *I'm* ... sorry, I ... [*Pause.*] When did this happen?

A: Two days ago.

B: The day after I moved in?

A: Yes. [*Pause.*] When I woke up that morning. I knew.

B: Aha. So, while I was out getting the *paper*, or—?

A: I know, I know it's not rational. I know that. And I know what I should do, I should wait, I'm supposed to wait, to see if *maybe* it's just some sort of weird *adjustment* thing or—

B: It *is*, that's what it *is*—

A: *I* know it's not, but even so, I'm supposed to wait so there's at least the *appearance*, so that you can look at it, so that people can look at it, from the *outside*, so the *story* makes sense, and say, "Well, they lived together for a while, and it didn't work out." Not *this* way, which looks *crazy:* "He moved in, she *asked* him to move in, and *then* she kicked him out, like, *instantly*, she's obviously *nuts*!" But I have to. Anyway.

B: But, so, then . . . Why *did* you ask me to move in?

A: Well, gee, I obviously had no idea this would happen.

B: I see, so, *you* can be sarcastic, but—

A: No, just! I guess . . . I thought that I was getting something else.

B: What? What else? You *know* me, we've . . . I mean . . .

A: I thought I was *getting* you. You who doesn't live here.

B: I'm still me.

A: No. You're not. You can't be you who doesn't live here because now you *do* so now you're you who *does* live here.

B: Are you *drunk* or something?

A: I'm *fucking serious.*

B: I . . . know that.

[*Pause.*]

A: I thought I was getting what we already had. Only more. But that's not what you get. Is it.

B: No. [*Pause.*] It's not fair.

A: Yeah. I guess that's what I meant. [*Pause.*] God, my makeup must be all over my face.

B: Kinda.

A: I'm . . . so sorry.

B: It doesn't look so bad.

A: About *this.*

B: I know. [*Pause.*] But, hey, no. It's not like this was already the worst night of my life or anything. Oh, wait . . .

A [*a weak chuckle*]: Heh.

[*Pause.*]

B: So . . . do you want to go to this thing, or what?

A: Are you serious?

B: Of course. I'm taking you out.

A: Come on . . .

B: What?

A: You don't have to do that.

B: I do, actually. Otherwise I've thrown away sixty dollars.

A: You know what I mean. It's . . . You don't have to be *nice*.

B: Oh, I'm *not* being nice. You're going to *hate* this.

[A *laughs*.]

> I'm serious. It's exactly the kind of play you hate. I'm doing this to punish you. It's very experimental. Post-post-modern.

A: There's a post-*post*-modern now?

B: There's a post-post-*post*-modern. This guy's actually behind the times.

A: You're just trying to be sweet and make me laugh.

B: So?

A: So this is a tactic. To get me to change my mind.

B: What? No it's not. [*Pause.*] It's not. [*Pause.*] Why, is it working?

A: Hey . . .

B: Look, do you want to come? [*Pause.*] Come on. What do you say?

[A *turns to* B, *takes his hand, leans in as if to say something incredibly tender, and says:*]

A: Technical Instrument: Lighting i.e. "Next Cue" *Formal Device:* Fade i.e. "Lights Down Slowly" *Authorial Intent:* End First Scene.

[*Lights fade. In darkness,* A *continues to speak:*]

Technical Instrument: Lighting *Formal Device:* Bump i.e. "Lights Up Quickly" *Authorial Intent:* Begin Second Scene.

[*And we hear her recorded voice again.*]

[*Recorded*] Two.

2

[*Lights up.* A *is discovered seated at the counter, putting on makeup, exactly as before.*]

A: Design Instrument: Set plus Lighting *Formal Device:* Discovery i.e. "Living Room slash Kitchen Is Now Visible" *Authorial Intent:* Establishment of Physical World *Performative Instrument:* Actor i.e. Character "A" *Formal Device:* Discovery plus Activity i.e. "At lights up, A looks into a mirror and puts on makeup." *Authorial*

Intent: Introduction of Character A plus Manifestation of Central Metaphor

B [*from off*]: *Performative Instrument:* Actor i.e. Character "B" *Formal Device:* Entrance i.e. "Someone unlocks the door."

[B *enters.*]

"B Enters from the Hall." *Authorial Intent:* Introduction of Character B plus Establishment of Familiarity with Character A

[A *and* B *look at one another.*]

A AND B: *Formal Device:* Scene

B: *Authorial Intent:* Dramatization of Idea Resulting in Visceral Emotional Spectatorial Engagement plus Propagation of Same

A: *Formal Device:* Tactical Speech in Pursuit of Characterological Objectives

B: I.e. "Dialogue"

A: *Objective:* Greeting plus Kindness *Tactic:* Feigned Interest

B: *Objective:* Comfort *Tactic:* Complaint i.e. "Worst night of my life." *Authorial Intent:* Humorous Establishment of Hyperbolically Negative Self-Assessment Unintentionally Concordant with Imminent Reality i.e. "Setup"

A: *Objective:* Confirm That All Is Well plus Quell Fear That Character "B" Is Aware of Secret Truth *Tactic:* Expression of Concern plus Nonexpression of Deeper Concern

[B *exits to the bedroom.*]

B [*as he goes*]: *Device:* Exit

A: *Intent:* Contrast Purposeless Movement with Purposeful Stillness

[B *returns.*]

B: *Instrument:* Costume *Device:* Costume Change i.e. "B returns without his jacket and tie." *Objective:* Permission to Tell Lengthy Story *Tactic:* Insistence upon Lack of Desire to Tell Lengthy Story

A: *Objective:* Not to Hear Lengthy Story *Tactic:* Acceptance of Clearly Disingenuous Lack of Desire to Tell Lengthy Story

B: *Objective:* Comfort plus Further Intertwining of Lives *Tactic:* Begin Lengthy Story *Formal Device:* Detailed Reportage of Offstage Events i.e. "Greek Messenger"

A: *Objective:* Stop Story *Tactic:* Indication i.e. "A looks oddly at B, but says nothing."

B: *Objective:* Prevent A from Staring *Tactic:* Stop Story plus Find Slippers *Authorial Intent:* Expositional Establishment of Recentness of B's Arrival as Permanent Inhabitant of A's Kitchen slash Living Room

A: *Objective:* Prevent Line of Questioning Regarding Odd Look *Tactic:* Urge Continuation of Lengthy Story *Authorial Intent:* That Attempted Avoidance Lead Ironically to Displaced Confrontation with That Which Is Being Avoided i.e.:

B: "Are you happy?"

A: "I guess . . . that's a good question."

[B *exits to the bedroom.*]

B [*as he goes*]: *Device:* Exit *Intent:* To Conclude Story Dramatically for Heightened Impact plus Create Expectation of Third Exit-to-Come in Concordance with Deeply Ingrained "Rule of Three"

A: *Objective:* Delay *Tactic:* Keep the Story Going Keep the Story Going Keep the—

[B *returns.*]

B [*reading*]: "In order to do what I wanted to do for the rest of my life I had to learn so much about it that I ruined forever my ability to enjoy it in the way that made me want to do it in the first place." *Authorial Intent:* That Narrative Particulars of Reported Events Echo Spectatorially Witnessed Events i.e. "Layering" a.k.a. "Metaphor"

[*Pause.*]

A: *Objective:* Convince Us Both It Is Not True *Tactic:* Insistence

B: *Objective:* To Be Convinced *Tactic:* Request a More Persuasive Tactic

A: *Objective:* Change the Subject i.e. "Can we not talk about this anymore?"

B: *Tactic:* Acquiescence

A: *Tactic:* Attack Bathroom Clutter

B: *Tactic:* Apologize for Bathroom Clutter

A: *Tactic:* Pause Meaningfully with Lipstick in Hand

B: "Shit. Right. Yes." *Device:* Third Exit

A: *Objective:* Fight Back Tears *Tactic:* Tell Him It's Fine It's Completely Fine Everything Is Fine It's Totally—

[B *returns.*]

B: *Tactic:* Change

A: *Objective:* Don't Cry *Tactic:* Cry

[A *begins to cry.*]

B: *Tactic:*—

A: *Objective:* Freedom from These Feelings *Tactic:* Truth

B: "What? [*Pause.*] Yes you do."

A: *Authorial Intent:* Raising of Stakes

B: *Super-Objective:* Warm-Safe Shelter plus Available Sustenance plus Frequent Opportunities to Mate with Fertile Partner plus Lifelong Comfort i.e. "Survival"

A: *Super-Objective:* The Freedom to Seek Out True Super-Objective i.e. "Survival"

B: *Objective:* Make Her Stay

A: *Objective:* Make Him Let Me Go

B: *Device:* Silence *Authorial Intent:* Convey That Words Are Insufficient at Times like This

[*Pause.*]

A: *Device:* Explicit Reference to Physical Manifestation of Central Metaphor in Collapse slash Acknowledgment of Divine slash Authorial Power i.e. "God, my makeup must be all over my face." *Authorial Intent:* Convey That End of Scene slash Relationship Is Near

B: *Objective:* Change Her Mind *Tactic:* Behave in a Manner Designed to Change Her Mind

A: "There's a post-*post*-modern now?"

B: *Objective:* Change Her Mind *Tactic:* Insist Behavior Is Not a Tactic Designed to Change Her Mind

A: *Objective:* [*Pause.*] Unknown

B: *Tactic:* Explicit Interrogative with Multiple Meanings i.e. "Come on. What do you say?" *Authorial Intent:* End Scene with Open-Ended Question So That . . .

[A *turns to* B *and takes his hand as she speaks.*]

A: *Technical Instrument:* Lighting i.e. "Next Cue" *Formal Device:* Fade i.e. "Lights Down Slowly" . . .

[*Lights fade as* A *continues with her repetition of the final line of the first scene, but her voice is soon drowned out by recorded voices, playing in darkness, first hers, then his, overlapping into a cacophony that sonically swallows the scene:*]

[*Recorded*] *Authorial Intent:* Convey Shift of Formal Conventions from Naturalistic slash Realist i.e. "Living Room slash Kitchen" to Post-Post-Modern i.e. "Living Room slash Kitchen Where Meaning Is Swallowed by Awareness of Awareness That Kitchen Is Not Kitchen." *Tactic:* Transition to Newly Invented Form of Dialogue Triggering Lights Up on Second Scene—

B [*recorded, overlapping*]: *Formal Device:* Second Scene Swallows Itself in Endless Introspective Loop *Authorial Intent:* Convey End of Second Scene via Description of Description of Description of Description of Description of—

A [*recorded, continuous*]: Three.

3

[*Lights up.* A *is discovered seated at the counter, at the mirror. This time, however, she is removing her makeup. She counts quietly along with the number of times she wipes each disposable makeup remover cloth against her face.*]

A: Four. Five. Six. Seven. Eight. Nine. Ten.

[A *throws the cloth into the sink and pulls a new one out of a box on the counter.*]

One. Two. Three.

[*Blackout. In darkness.*]

Hey! I'm still in here! [*Pause.*] Hello?

[*Lights up.* B *enters through the closet, which, of course, has the effect of completely violating the reality of the space. We can see "backstage" through the open door.* B *wears jeans and a T-shirt and has a bag with the name of the theater in which the play is being performed slung across his shoulder. He is holding a bouquet.*]

B: Hey, sorry, it's just me. I didn't realize anyone was still here.

A: Well, I am.

B: Good show tonight, by the way.

A: Yeah?

B: Yeah.

A: Well shit. Thanks. You too.

B: You don't have to say that just because I said it.

A: No, I mean it, _____* you're pretty fuckin' good.

B: Well, cool. Thank you, _____.

A [looking to the flowers]: Girlfriend come see you tonight?

B: What? Oh. No. Parents.

A: They flew in for *this*?

B: The train. It's only about an hour. So.

A: Well. That's nice.

B: Actually, I don't *have* a girlfriend.

A: Okay.

B: You never asked.

A: I know I didn't.

[*Pause.*]

B: Taking off your makeup?

*The blanks should be filled in with the actual names of the actors.

A: Dude, it takes for-fucking-ever. I spend *the whole play* putting it on, *after* I've already put it on before the play, so there's a layer like eighteen inches thick on my face by the time the thing is over.

B: Why are you doing it out here?

A: "The bathroom's all cluttered with your stuff."

B: Haha. Right. No, why really?

A: I like to get out of character on stage. It's like a ritual.

B: Huh. That's . . . uh . . .

A: It's weird, I know.

B: It's not weird.

A: No, that's okay, it's fucking weird.

B: It's kind of cool.

A: How is it cool?

B: I'm always just sort of . . . show up, do my thing . . . I've never been one of those actors who like, you know, "Oh, I have to touch the doorknob six times before I go out on stage or else . . ."

A: Which is weird.

B: No no no, I always was sort of jealous of those actors because, like . . . they have this . . . or . . . I don't know.

A: Okay. Well, nice try, but you're shitting me, and I'm totally aware of how fucking stupid it is.

B: You swear a lot.

[*Pause.*]

A: What?

B: I don't have a problem with it. I'm just saying. You say the word "fuck" like . . . really a *lot.*

A [*uncertainly*]: Well . . . I guess . . .

B: It's just something I noticed.

A: Maybe I should be more like her.

B: Who?

A: Character A.

B: Oh. Well—

A: Right, like that *big* moment, where she says, she's all emotional, and she says, "I'm fucking serious!" It's this *huge* thing, like, we know how fucking *huge* it is, because she *swears,* oh my fucking *god,* right?

B: You don't like her.

A: If she were a real person I do not think that she and I would be the best of friends, no. [*Beat.*] But, I mean, don't get me wrong, it's a good *part.* It's a fine *part.* [*Beat.*] Fuck: it's a *part.* [*Beat.*] And, hey, she's not quite as big of a pussy as you.

B: Hey, now—

A: Your character, I mean.

[*She's taken out a cigarette.*]

Mind if I . . . ?

[B *shakes his head.* A *begins to smoke.*]

B: I don't know. I think they're both kind of . . . I think they're sort of . . .

A: What?

B: Never mind. [*Pause.*] In case you couldn't tell I'm not very articulate.

A: Shut up. Yes you are.

B: No, you just think that.

A: Why would I "just think" that?

B: No, it's okay, it's kind of my . . . thing.

A: What is?

B: Like playing guys who are way smarter or who talk way better than I do. Like who the playwright sees *himself* as? Because of how I look maybe? Like, I'm not hand-some, not really a leading man type of guy, and I can *play* really smart, and kind of angsty and neurotic. So that's what I get to do. It's my thing.

A: You're totally handsome.

B: Well, okay. I mean: thanks, _____. But not in *that* way. You know?

A: Yeah. I do know. I'm also . . . not in *that* way.

B: Oh you so are.

A: Whatever.

[*She gestures to him.*]

The *point* . . . ?

B: I'm not as smart as my lack of good looks might have you believe.

[*Beat.*]

A: *That* was pretty smart.

B: A playwright friend of mine gave me that one.

A: Ah.

B: In fact . . . Could I tell you something?

A: Go.

B: That whole second scene I don't have any idea what I'm talking about.

A: Really?

B: Not a clue. I know the director explained it to us eighty times—

A: Yeah, she did.

B: But I just, I don't . . . And I had the *worst* time *memorizing* it.

A: Oh, well yeah, me too.

B: Right?

A: I mean, it's not fucking English. How are you supposed to attach the *meaning* to it that makes it even *possible* to, to—

B: Let me show you something.

[B *maybe goes to the couch or something, lifts a pillow, and pulls out the script.*]

A: Shut up! Is that the script?

B: Just the second scene. I don't have any problem with the first scene, like you said, it's in English. But this, I—

A: No, I *know*, it's . . . Here, check this out . . .

[A *perhaps opens the refrigerator and pulls out another copy of the script.*]

B: Hey!

A: I know!

B: That is so funny!

A: God, can you imagine, if we both blanked on it at the same time?

B: Right, we each pull out the script and just start . . . like—

A: No one would probably *notice*. By the middle of that scene, fucking *anything* that happens, they'll just think it's a part of the show.

B: Right, like—

A: Equipment could start falling from above and like I could be lying on the stage bleeding from my head and they'd be like:

[*She applauds.*]

"Hooray! Encore! Genius!"

B: Yeah, it's really . . . uh . . . Yeah. [*Pause.*] What are you doing now?

A: You mean next?

B: Well—

A: Next I'm doing a commercial for nicotine patches. And then I'm playing Ophelia in Texas. Hoo. Talk about a pussy.

B: Okay. No, but, I mean: *now*. Tonight. When you leave here.

A: Oh, I guess . . . going back to the cheap-ass hotel they have us in. Right?*

B: Do you want to maybe grab a drink?

[*Pause.*]

A: Uh-oh.

B: What?

A: "*Objective:* Fucking."

B: Whoa—

A: "*Tactic:* Inebriation."

B: I'm not . . . Hey, just a *drink*, it's an *expression*. You could drink . . . *milk*—

A: I don't date people I'm in shows with. And I also don't date *actors*, in general, too many bad experiences, so that's two strikes right there—

B: No, no, look, I just think you're really smart. And *really* talented. And sort of . . . beautiful and fascinating. That's not so terrible.

A: "*Tactic:* Flattery."

B: It's true!

A: "*Tactic:*—"

*If the play is being performed in New York City, this line should read as follows: "Oh, I guess . . . going back to my apartment in Queens."

B: Stop it! Stop that! Jesus. Not everything is . . . *fake.*

A: I know that, _____, and I like it that way, which is why I stopped dating actors, as a result of the aforementioned bad experiences.

B: *I'm* not like that. If you got to *know* me . . . *I* want to get to know *you.*

A: See, no, that's the thing. That's the thing I figured out about these . . . shows. You go to some city, where you don't *know* anybody, and there's nothing to *do,* and you're spending all your time with this small group of people who are generally charming and funny and good *performers,* and even the ones who are maybe not handsome in "that" way are totally handsome, because they're in a job where people have to *look* at them all the time, so they know how to make themselves nice to look at, and out of *necessity* you feel: yes, I would like to get to know this person better. But it's like clockwork, you take your bows closing night, and you have that little party, and you get on the train the next day, and it's just *gone.* It's not a feeling that . . . that *blooms* with someone that you meet doing a show, the . . . the show *is* the feeling. And when the show is over, *that's* over, too. You don't want to get to know me. You only think you do. So let's just leave it at that, because that's a nice feeling you're having right now, and . . . sure, I'm having it too, okay? Happy? And it's a hell of a lot nicer than the feelings we'd start having once we *did* get to know each other, because the better we did, the worse it would get.

So let's just . . . I *like* you, I am *attracted* to you, I think you're talented and you're *very* sweet, and . . . Let's just leave it at that. [*Pause.*] Okay?*

B: Can't argue with that.

A: That's right. You can't.

B: You've got it all pretty much figured out.

A: Yes. I do.

B: And just so you know, I don't date actresses. As a general rule. Too.

[*Pause.*]

A: Oh. So, why—?

B: Because: what if I'm wrong? What if . . . in this case . . . if I got to know *you* better, you specifically I'm saying . . . What if it was . . . sure, messier maybe, yeah, more, uh, more *difficult*, but, like . . . It might be harder to know what it means, but it also might be more . . . meaningful.

A: Nice. Your playwright friend give you that line?

B: It's . . . not a line. I'm just me here. [*Pause.*] Look, let's go somewhere else. Just to talk more. Somewhere . . . [*gesturing to the set*] out of *here*.

---

*In New York, cut the phrases "You go to some city, where you don't *know* anybody, and there's nothing to *do*, and" and "and you get on the train the next day."

A: _____.

B: _____. [*Pause.*] Come on. [*Pause.*] What do you say?

[*A moment.* B *looks at* A.]

[*The* READER *appears again.*]

READER: Four. Szinhaz.*

[*A transition begins as there is the sound of recorded applause. Perhaps the* READER *sits in the audience for the next play.*]

*The pronunciation is Sēn'-has (as in "*has* been").

FOUR

SZINHAZ

[*Two chairs. In one sits* ISTVAN, *bearded, wearing black. In the other sits* MARIE, *lovely, holding a stack of index cards.*]

MARIE: Hello, Americans. Welcome very much to our special talk today talking with the very special and interesting director Istvan Zoltan Andras.* Who will talk with us about his work which is some of the most special and interesting work in the whole of former Soviet Union. Some of it that we will be talking about will be in not English. When he is speaking. And I will try to make it for you in English. And my English is very bad. It will be for you very painful. For you to listen to it. But if you try, hopefully, you will get used to it.

Okay! So! Here sitting next to me now is, you know him, and who is he already, which is the reason you are coming here, but I will say one things or two things about him also in case of you forgot it.

He is borned beneath the Soviets at what was a very bad and terrible time in which there was no freedoms. And this was very very painful. For him and for all of us. But we got used to it.

---

* The pronunciation is Ēsht'-van (with –*van* rhyming with *man*) Zōl'-tan Awn'-drash.

Next, after he growed up some little bits, he wented through training at our *Theatre Institute of Academy of Drama Studies*. Here a director is practicing first by working very much in a room alone with no actors.

After this, Istvan is starting his own company, the name of it, in English, it's not so easy, em, *The Slow Death of the Human Soul*. This company is now of course very much knowed about by peoples, but for very much time it was not knowed, or if it was, it was unliked, and not liked, which is what people were saying in the audiences, and in the critics, and also shouting in the streets at Istvan. Until he growed up some little bits more and made his very special production of a play by Anton Pavlovich Chekhov, who, you know who is he, of his play, em, *There Are Sisters and There Are Three of Them*. Yes? And this production have such realism that it make his reputation for genius. But because Istvan does not care by now about this, by now, and so was unable to enjoy it, this success, too, he found very painful.

Okay! So! I have here the questions that you wroted down for him before. On index card. And because Istvan can hear English more better than he can speak it, I will read it loud, and he can think about it. And then he will answer. And I will say for you.

[MARIE *looks at the index card on the top of the pile.*]

MARIE: The question is: "Have you ever and or would you ever direct outside of your own company?"

[ISTVAN *speaks in his own language. Her translations can overlap slightly with his speech, organically, as needed, sometimes checking in with him—whatever feels right.*]

MARIE: Yes, Istvan has worked without *The Slow Death of the Human Soul* three times. And each time it was very different from the other times.

[ISTVAN *speaks in his own language.*]

MARIE: The first time it was in Vienna with a very special and interesting company there called *Time Will Destroy Your Capacity to Love.*

[ISTVAN *speaks in his own language.*]

MARIE: And it was terrible.

[ISTVAN *speaks in his own language.*]

MARIE: It was like being punched.

[ISTVAN *speaks in his own language.*]

MARIE: Again and again and again.

[ISTVAN *speaks in his own language.*]

MARIE: Into his face.

[ISTVAN *speaks in his own language.*]

MARIE: By a train.

[ISTVAN *speaks in his own language.*]

MARIE: And this was because this company is having its own director who is with Istvan, em, rivalizating? Yes? They are making rivals with each other? And Istvan cannot work this way. Rivalizating with another man.

[ISTVAN *speaks in his own language.*]

MARIE: And so was exposed in front of collaborators and later audiences to only, em, humiliation.

[ISTVAN *speaks in his own language.*]

MARIE: And ridicule.

[ISTVAN *speaks in his own language.*]

MARIE: And also, how do you call them, projectiles.

[ISTVAN *speaks in his own language.*]

MARIE: Which was at first very painful.

[ISTVAN *speaks in his own language.*]

MARIE: But he got used to it.

[ISTVAN *speaks in his own language.*]

MARIE: The second time it was in Italy. In Roma.

[ISTVAN *speaks in his own language.*]

MARIE: And this time it was horrible.

[ISTVAN *speaks in his own language.*]

MARIE: Like being kicked in his groins.

[ISTVAN *speaks in his own language.*]

MARIE: Forever.

[ISTVAN *speaks in his own language.*]

MARIE: And this was because the actors inside Italy could not understand what Istvan is telling to them.

[ISTVAN *speaks in his own language.*]

MARIE: So they do whatever it is that they want.

[ISTVAN *speaks in his own language.*]

MARIE: And also there is much money and a big stage and big things flying.

[ISTVAN *speaks in his own language.*]

MARIE: But all of it means nothing.

[ISTVAN *speaks in his own language.*]

MARIE: And this was very painful.

[ISTVAN *speaks in his own language.*]

MARIE: But he got used to it.

[ISTVAN *speaks in his own language.*]

MARIE: The third time was the most different of all. When he goes to Moscow.

[ISTVAN *speaks in his own language.*]

MARIE: And this was extremely bad.

[*A moment.* ISTVAN *doesn't say anything else. A moment.* MARIE *moves the index card to the back of the pile. She reads the new one on top. She glances at* ISTVAN *and back at the cards. She moves the new card to the back. She reads the next one and moves it to the back. Finally she sees one she likes.*]

MARIE: The question is: "I saw your Chekhov production last winter. And I was intrigued by how you were able to work without a set or any other design elements and also to eliminate much of the text. Why did you make this choice?"

[ISTVAN *speaks in his own language.*]

MARIE: Our play last winter was the Chekhov, em, *The Animal Which Is Flying in Circles over the Ocean but Near to the Beach . . . ? And Enjoys Garbage and Is a Kind of a Bird . . . ?* Yes? You know it? So this was the play.

[ISTVAN *speaks in his own language.*]

MARIE: First when we are working on it he thinks that we will require lights and sound noises and things like this that one will have most of the time.

[ISTVAN *speaks in his own language.*]

MARIE: But then he realized something.

[ISTVAN *speaks in his own language.*]

MARIE: Oh! Which he will demonstrate by taking right now a small pause in front of you.

[ISTVAN *speaks in his own language.*]

MARIE: A small silence.

[ISTVAN *speaks in his own language.*]

MARIE: In which there will be no talking in it.

ISTVAN: Now.

[*A silence. Long enough to feel it. However long feels like it might be too long and a little longer than that. They don't move. Then, at last, finally,* ISTVAN *speaks in his own language.*]

MARIE: Okay! So!

[ISTVAN *speaks in his own language.*]

MARIE: This silence that we just have. It is very boring.

[ISTVAN *speaks in his own language.*]

MARIE: Probably you are very bored during it and while it is going on.

[ISTVAN *speaks in his own language.*]

MARIE: Or perhaps after a few moments you began to fantasize sexually.

[ISTVAN *speaks in his own language.*]

MARIE: He did.

[ISTVAN *speaks in his own language. A moment.* MARIE *speaks back to him, gently scolding.* ISTVAN *insists, in his own language, that she translate. She sighs.*]

MARIE: He thought about this woman here in the first row, hello, and how much and in how many different ways he would like to make love with her.

[ISTVAN *speaks in his own language. A moment.*]

MARIE: Perhaps finishing with an ejaculation.

[ISTVAN *repeats his last few words. The translation was incomplete.*]

MARIE: Into her face.

[ISTVAN *speaks in his own language.*]

MARIE: Which at first might be painful.

[ISTVAN *speaks in his own language.*]

MARIE: But she will get used to it.

[ISTVAN *speaks in his own language.*]

MARIE: And so this was very entertaining to think about it.

[ISTVAN *speaks in his own language.*]

MARIE: But it was necessary. Because the small silence that we had here was too boring to exist inside of it without feeling, how do you say it . . . ? A stillness in the earth that deprives us of all meaning. Yes?

[ISTVAN *speaks in his own language.*]

MARIE: But now he will tell you few things.

[ISTVAN *speaks in his own language.*]

MARIE: Probably you think that I, sitting here next to him, am here only to translate, and am selected because I know some small bad English, and also it is pleasing to look on me.

[ISTVAN *speaks in his own language.*]

MARIE: But actually I am also one of the actress in Istvan company so that I work with him and was his Nina in the play of the *Garbage Bird,* and one also of the *Triangle of Sisters,* and so on, so on.

[ISTVAN *speaks in his own language.* MARIE *sighs. She knows better than to object.*]

MARIE: And also we are lovers.

[ISTVAN *speaks in his own language.*]

MARIE: For many many years.

[ISTVAN *speaks in his own language.*]

MARIE: Since I am first working with him he loves me from my audition.

[ISTVAN *speaks in his own language.*]

MARIE: Which he remembers it so clear like it is happening still now.

[ISTVAN *speaks in his own language.*]

MARIE: He loves me so much.

[ISTVAN *speaks in his own language.*]

MARIE: He did not know it was possible so much to love a person.

[ISTVAN *speaks in his own language.*]

MARIE: And, in truth, when he was young, he was without any talent whatsoever, and he only make himself into himself for me, to become one that he thinks I can love.

[ISTVAN *speaks in his own language.*]

MARIE: And so never can there be for him work again or love again apart from he looks on me and sees me.

[ISTVAN *speaks in his own language.* MARIE *looks at* ISTVAN. *Then she turns back.*]

MARIE: But there is problem.

[ISTVAN *speaks in his own language.*]

MARIE: And. It is problem that I think he does not know.

[ISTVAN *speaks in his own language.*]

MARIE: But he knows it.

[ISTVAN *speaks in his own language. A small silence.* MARIE *says something very quietly to* ISTVAN. *He stares at her, impassive. A moment.*]

MARIE: That I am being with also another man.

[ISTVAN *speaks in his own language.*]

MARIE: One of the actors of the company.

[ISTVAN *speaks in his own language.*]

MARIE: From some months now. Maybe even from a whole year. He does not know exact the time.

[ISTVAN *speaks in his own language.*]

MARIE: And that I am falling perhaps in love with this man.

[ISTVAN *speaks in his own language.*]

MARIE: This man who he, Istvan, brought together with me, in many scenes, and using his skill to make for us a connection.

[ISTVAN *speaks in his own language.*]

MARIE: Causing this horrible disaster for himself.

[ISTVAN *speaks in his own language.*]

MARIE: He knows this. And now I know it that he knows it.

[ISTVAN *speaks in his own language.*]

MARIE: And now he gives to me a choice.

[ISTVAN *speaks in his own language.*]

MARIE: That I can stay with this man. And both of us will be made to go away from the company.

[ISTVAN *speaks in his own language.*]

MARIE: Or to stay with the company. But to stop with the other man and to love only Istvan.

[ISTVAN *speaks in his own language.*]

MARIE: And now he would like to make a second pause now.

[ISTVAN *speaks in his own language.*]

MARIE: To see how this one feels.

[ISTVAN *speaks in his own language.*]

MARIE: Not like a soul frozen.

[ISTVAN *speaks in his own language.*]

MARIE: But with motion forward for the soul.

[ISTVAN *speaks in his own language.*]

MARIE: Which, even though this motion is toward, how do you call . . . ? The endless grave? This movement, it is better than the stillness of the other pause before.

[ISTVAN *speaks in his own language.*]

MARIE: That it cannot be escaped.

[ISTVAN *speaks in his own language.*]

MARIE: But that there is no reason to escape it.

[ISTVAN *speaks in his own language.*]

MARIE: And yes. It will be very painful.

[ISTVAN *speaks in his own language.* MARIE *looks at him. She shakes her head. She looks away from him. A long silence. He stares at her. She stares away. Finally she turns back and looks at him.*]

[*The* READER *appears again.*]

READER: Five.

[*A transition begins . . .*]

FIVE

UNTITLED SHORT PLAY

[*Lights up on a table at a café. A* MAN *and a* WOMAN *sit across from each other. Off to the side is the* READER.]

READER: Untitled Short Play. [*Pause.*] Lights up on a table at a café. A man and a woman sit across from each other. They sit in silence for a moment. They are not looking at one another. [*Pause.*] But it's an avoidance borne not of unfamiliarity but more of something like the opposite, something like too much familiarity, or uncertainty about what, exactly, at this moment, their familiarity means, and so there is an awkwardness between them, a tension.

[*Pause. He looks over at them. A beat. He turns back to the audience.*]

There is clearly history here, is the point. The specifics or details or exact *particulars* of that history are not of course entirely clear from this opening image, but that these particulars exist is unmistakable, and their importance, the weight, or, maybe more accurately, the almost unbearable *meaning* of the particulars hangs over the table. Like a dense fog.

[He starts to look over but turns back almost immediately. At some point during the following, perhaps he starts to move around the space some.]

Which, while, okay, admittedly, being a pretty unremarkable not to say obvious simile to choose is on the other hand not an inappropriate one because what's most painful here, for both of them, is their inability to see inside each other, to know for sure whether all or even any of the aforementioned particulars which are of such importance to each of them individually are of some or even any importance to the person across the table, if they even care. Such that he might be thinking, "I remember the time we went for breakfast near my place and I was upset," this, just to interject into his thought, this being shortly after it all started, the beginning of what is now their shared history, a history which ended, like nearly all such histories, in a series of ambiguous encounters of entirely unclear parameters that became increasingly uncomfortable until they absolutely needed to stop, rendering their story, such as it is, one of those with a beginning, and then basically no middle, and then an ending, followed by a lengthy silence, which is, presumably at this very moment, about to be broken. *[Beat.]* Oh, but during the very tail end of which silence he's thinking back to an earlier and now bafflingly uncomplicated-seeming time, thinking, "I was having a bad morning, just in that way people sometimes wake up in a deadened place, in a certain emotional area where things have sort of lost their taste and luster a little, that seem to come *especially,* for me at least," this is him thinking, by the way, it's him who's thinking the word "me," "*especially* for me," he thinks, "in those times when I am most supposed to be or expected to be or what have you in a good or even ecstatic place like for instance after spending the night with somebody new, about whom I have felt up to this point relatively excited in a way that has been refreshing, but maybe this morning I turned a corner not to a lack of excitement about her, no, not exactly, but just to a place from which I am able to glimpse the fact that, no, after all, and of course, she will not actually be the solution to all of my problems that it seemed she might be, she will simply *be present* during some of them, meaning my problems, and of course this bad mood which itself derived from a realization that bad moods around her are even possible is *itself* the first example of this." He thinks. And he thinks, "But what I did is, hoping it would just pass, and never return, I hid it, and then it did pass, and then I told her about it later, once I was in a good mood again, the following week, and that made her sad, and she told me, 'Okay, look, don't be afraid to be sad in front of me, because I like you, not just you when you're happy, so you just go ahead and be yourself.' " He might be thinking that. And this memory is terrifying, because what if, and he has no way of knowing, she is by now no longer interested in his sadness, or, even worse, and more to the point, is no longer at all dismayed at the prospect of being shut out of his sadness, because to be close to him in that way no longer matters or appeals or occurs to her, that his even worrying about it might be simply annoying and a little scary and just a sign that he has held onto something or remains in the grip of something that seems now silly or distant or dismissible to her, the thought of which is painful enough that it makes him kind of wish that the whole thing had never started at all in the first place. The final irony being that, at the time, which is to say at the time of the original memory, this increased closeness actually *scared* him, actually kind of scared him, because he wasn't sure he was ready, et cetera, fear of intimacy, and so on, a sense of being trapped, blah blah blah, and that, while it is partly the result of that earlier fear and the effect it had on some of his behavior that to some extent created this distance, i.e. by triggering the aforementioned discomfort leading to e.g. the afore-mentioned ambiguity and resultant silence, that now the increased distance *is* what scares him. That, both, in their own time, are scary, and from both places he has the sense of gazing, wistfully, and with longing, at the other place. All of which accounts for why he hasn't even looked at her. And for why he has not spoken.

[*A moment. He starts to walk away. But he stops again.*]

She hasn't spoken yet, either, of course, and she might be thinking something similar, and have basically the same fear that he does, or she might be thinking pre-cisely what he most fears she's thinking, but, frankly, god only knows what the hell she's thinking, if he knew what she was thinking there would have been no reason to sit down and try to write this play, would there, and, in fact, earlier, when describing what hangs in the air between them, sort of unimaginatively, as a "fog," having at the time used the phrase "what is so painful for both of them" now seems in retrospect like a transparent attempt to pretend that an individual writer is actually capable of having more than one perspective, or of investing any perspective but the one that more or less approximates his own with anything other than the most superficial qualities, resulting in work filled with so-called characters who are actually just tissue-thin cartoons built mostly from lazy guesswork, I mean, Jesus Christ, what the hell are you thinking, what are you thinking over there, I have absolutely no idea, I could make something *up*, I could give you *words*, I could even draw to the best of my ability on remembered conversations and use actual words that you actually said, but that would be like painting a dollar sign on a balloon and saying it's a bag of money, okay, now *that's* a simile, thank you, but, anyway, the point is, I would just be hoping that by mimicking what I observed to be true, externally, that I could fool everyone, and that nobody would notice the fact that I don't have the faintest idea what might be going on inside there. Like, at all. And there is an analogous and equally insurmountable problem with attempting to "write" the other character, *him*, because an *awareness* of what's going on inside does not necessarily translate, especially given the limitations of the form, into an ability to *articulate* it in a way that allows words to match feeling, I mean what the hell am I going to write? "Lights up. Hey. Hey. How are you? Fine. You? Okay. You look well." It makes me want to take out my eyeballs with a grapefruit spoon, one of those cushy "scenes" in which every word is a step not *toward* but *away from* the dangerous truths that got it started, every fraudulent fucking word of it actually cloaking me more and more in safety when the whole point was to be, for one second, just kind of *naked*, in the stinging wind. I sat down here to re-create the closeness. And the very first keystroke begins to re-create the distance. All of which, taken together, seems to defeat the whole point of writing this, which, naturally, is to express these things truthfully, and, on some level, to express them specifically to *you*, insofar as this short play, the one about those two people over there, will be performed, and there will be an audience, and that audience might very well include you, and how on earth could some lame scene where two people just talk to each other get more than thimble-deep into anything that remotely resembles *anything* that even comes within a country mile of an approximation of the barest outline of the feelings that gave rise to the need to write this, how can it do what it is *meant* to do, which is reach out, just reach out from the stage, grab you by the lapels, figuratively speaking, unless you happen to be wearing lapels, and just shout in your face: "Tell me I did not make a terrible mistake. Tell me there is absolutely nothing I could have done. Tell me I wasn't supposed to fight harder. Please please please please tell me that." [*Beat.*] *He* is thinking all of this by the way. The unnamed man wandering around the space saying these things is thinking this. Not me, safe, at home, at the keyboard, writing it. It's him who's using the word "I." Not me. [*Pause.*] The terrible thing about writing, the thing that, sometimes, he finds the most terrible is the way that that initial spark, that maybe orange glowing ember-tip of a new thing, that genesis, that it happens so easily, that the idea for something comes in a flash, which, while, okay, admittedly, is not a very original way to describe a moment of inspiration in the creative process, but it's true, it's almost literally true if you think of neurons and the way they make little electrical storms, but how an idea will come in a flash: A man and a woman. Sitting at a table. There is history. There are *particulars*. That comes, all of it, in a single moment. Or, okay, full disclosure, because that was never the idea, so, more accurately, to be really really truthful, the idea of a scene that doesn't get to start, because it is hijacked by its own opening stage direction, by someone nameless, identified only as "The Reader." This idea comes in a flash, and it's joyous, it seems right, and good, and like it will be, for as long as it takes to write, it will be the answer to all of my problems. He thinks. But how, and this, finally, is the terrible thing, how the process of actually writing it is nothing at all like that first flash. The rest is just the day-to-day work of building something. Often frustrating. Often boring. Often seeming to be almost entirely without the prospect of any discernible reward. And that the choices are therefore to write it and feel only deadened by the poor results especially in light of the brightness of the flash. Or not to write it. And to be haunted by it. A chance unruined because it went untried. An impossible choice unredeemed by the fact that even this, even this idea to write about the choice itself, making use of slightly more recently developed but no less contrived meta-formal meta-conventions, as a way of maybe, finally, saying something a little bit near the vicinity of what he wants to say, even this was part of the idea from the beginning. This was always the idea. [*Pause.*] And we never named it. And it was so brief. And, god, I miss you like crazy sometimes. Better never to begin.

[READER *is now looking at the table.* MAN *turns to look at* WOMAN, *who is still looking away, and opens his mouth to speak.*]

READER: Fade to black.

[*Lights fade on the café.* READER *looks out at audience for a few beats as if he is going to say something else. Then he speaks.*]

End of play.

[*Fade to black.*]